TALES OF HORROR
ALIENS

by Jim Pipe

BEARPORT
PUBLISHING

New York, New York

Credits

Amit Gogia CyberMedia Services: 24–25; Stephen Coburn: 22; Corbis: 7; Christian Darkin: 24; electricsoda: 10; Johanna Goodyear: 11; Chris Harvey: 8–9 (hands); Roman Krochuk: 29 (inset); Mary Evans Picture Library: 20; NASA Picture Library: 30–31, 31; Tyler Olsen: 20–21; Styve Reineck: 23; Rex Features: Cover, Title Page, 15; Science Photo Library: 16–17, 19 (inset); ticktock Media image archive: 4, 5, 13, 14, 18, 19, 26–27 (all), 28–29; Bora Ucack: 8–9 (clipboard).

Every effort has been made to trace the copyright holders and we apologize in advance for any unintentional omissions. We would be pleased to insert the appropriate acknowledgment in any subsequent edition of this publication.

Library of Congress Cataloging-in-Publication Data

Pipe, Jim, 1966-
  Aliens / by Jim Pipe.
      p. cm. – (Tales of horror)
  Includes index.
  ISBN-13: 978-1-59716-202-9 (library binding)
  ISBN-10: 1-59716-202-7 (library binding)
  ISBN-13: 978-1-59716-209-8 (pbk.)
  ISBN-10: 1-59716-209-4 (pbk.)
  1. Human-alien encounters–Juvenile literature. 2. Life on other planets–Juvenile literature.
I. Title. II. Series: Pipe, Jim, 1966- Tales of horror.

  BF2050.P55 2007
  001.942–dc22

                              2006014419

For more information, write to Bearport Publishing Company, Inc., 101 Fifth Avenue, Suite 6R, New York, New York 10003. Printed in the United States of America.

10 9 8 7 6 5 4 3 2 1

The Tales of Horror series was originally developed by ticktock Media Ltd.

Table of Contents

Is Anybody Out There? 4

UFOs. 6

Close Encounters. 8

Types of Aliens 10

Alien Abductions 12

Evidence of Aliens. 14

The Roswell Crash 16

Alien Hoaxes 18

Hot Spots. 20

Aliens in History. 22

Alien Fiction 24

Movie Aliens. 26

IFOs. 28

Do Aliens Exist?. 30

Glossary and Index. 32

Is Anybody Out There?

Our **galaxy** contains about 100 billion stars. Could one of them, like our sun, be a source of life to its planets?

Scientists are looking deep into space for signs of intelligent life. They believe other life is probably out there, somewhere. Yet could aliens from outer space really visit Earth? Are they here already?

Many people say they have seen or met **extraterrestrials**. Some say the aliens are small, gray creatures with black, glassy eyes. Other people say they look like hairy monsters with sharp, hungry teeth.

Most scientists do not believe that creatures from other planets have ever been on Earth. However, a few scientists do believe that aliens have visited. Who is right? Read on and then decide what you believe.

Visitors from Outer Space

Are aliens friendly or dangerous? It depends on whom you ask. Some people have claimed that aliens have kidnapped them. Others have described meeting friendly aliens, such as the movie alien, E. T.

UFOs

How could aliens reach our planet? Most likely spaceships, or **UFOs** (Unidentified Flying Objects), would bring them. Many people claim they have seen these spaceships.

The most commonly described UFO is called a **flying saucer**. It looks like two shiny saucers put together. People have been seeing this kind of spaceship for over 2,000 years. In 329 BC, the army of Alexander the Great was crossing a river into India. They claimed they saw "two silver shields" in the sky!

People have reported seeing UFOs that look like eggs, cigars, pyramids, and wheels of fire. Many scientists think these people are really just seeing **meteors** or airplane lights.

Proof of a UFO?

Betty and Barney Hill claimed they saw the inside of a spaceship in September of 1961. Later, Betty drew a star map, which she says she saw on the spaceship. It showed stars in another part of our galaxy. Eight years later, **astronomers** actually discovered this group of stars!

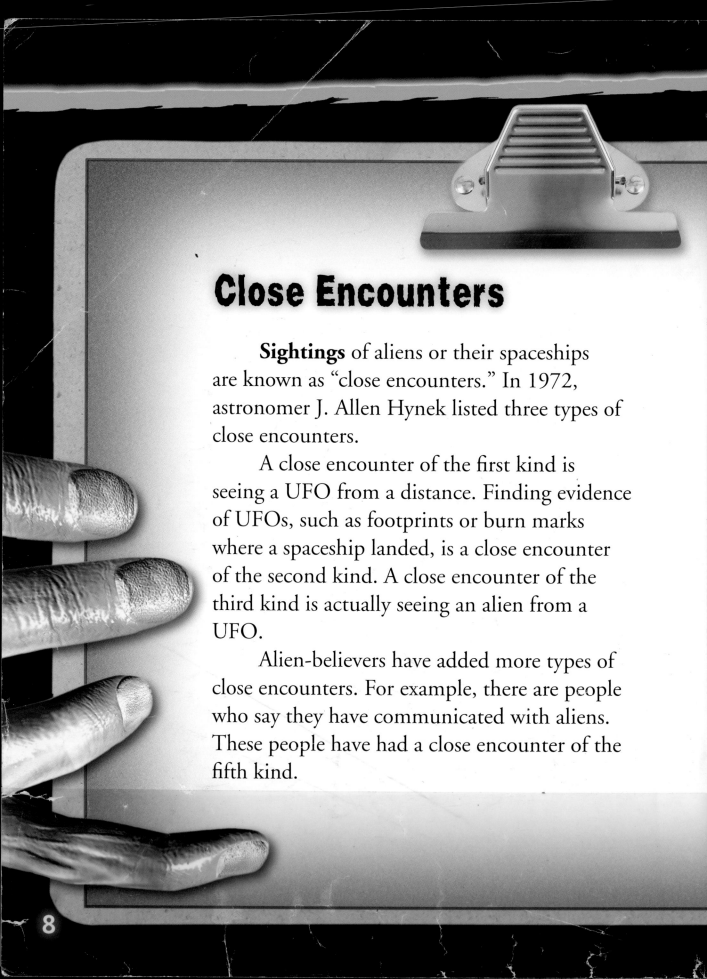

Close Encounters

Sightings of aliens or their spaceships are known as "close encounters." In 1972, astronomer J. Allen Hynek listed three types of close encounters.

A close encounter of the first kind is seeing a UFO from a distance. Finding evidence of UFOs, such as footprints or burn marks where a spaceship landed, is a close encounter of the second kind. A close encounter of the third kind is actually seeing an alien from a UFO.

Alien-believers have added more types of close encounters. For example, there are people who say they have communicated with aliens. These people have had a close encounter of the fifth kind.

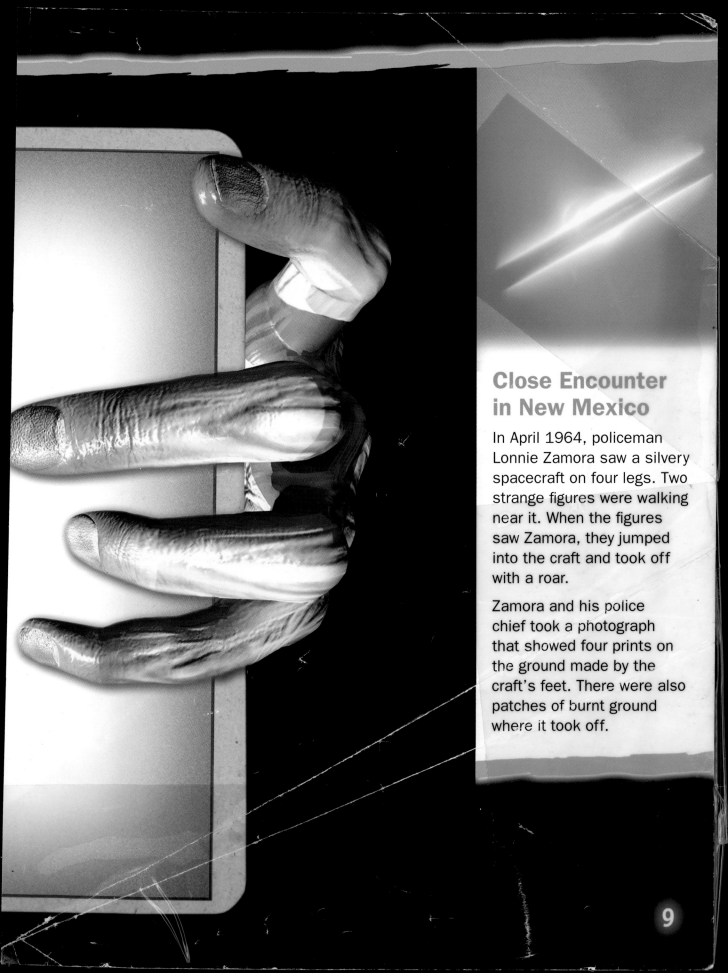

Close Encounter in New Mexico

In April 1964, policeman Lonnie Zamora saw a silvery spacecraft on four legs. Two strange figures were walking near it. When the figures saw Zamora, they jumped into the craft and took off with a roar.

Zamora and his police chief took a photograph that showed four prints on the ground made by the craft's feet. There were also patches of burnt ground where it took off.

Types of Aliens

What do aliens look like? People say they have seen aliens that look like humans, robots, worms, and giant insects. Many reports describe "little green men" with antennae on their heads.

Aliens come in different sizes. Some are huge. Others are so tiny they can worm their way into bodies and take them over.

The most commonly reported alien is the "gray." These aliens are about three-and-a-half feet (1 m) tall. They have a gray or silver body and a large head. Some have big, round eyes while others have thin slits.

Tall Aliens

In the 1950s and 1960s, many people claimed they saw Nordic aliens. These are tall aliens with blue eyes. They were usually peaceful. According to people at a sighting in 1953, some Nordic aliens came to warn humans of invading gray aliens.

Alien Abductions

Many people believe they have been taken aboard alien ships against their will. This kidnapping is called alien **abduction**. In most cases, people believe they were kidnapped so that aliens could study them.

Researchers say most victims tell similar stories of their abductions. Often the victims are "missing time." They can't remember where they were for days, hours, even weeks. Victims may also have strange scars or burns on their bodies. They cannot remember how the marks got there.

Victims also usually complain of having nightmares about aliens. Others have a nagging feeling that they have met an alien. Most saw a UFO before they were abducted.

The Travis Walton Story

In November 1975, seven men who were working in a forest saw a UFO. One of the men, Travis Walton, went to investigate.

Walton was **paralyzed** by a beam of light from the UFO. His friends ran away, thinking he was dead! Walton's body then disappeared. Five days later, Walton turned up in a nearby town. Under **hypnosis** he remembered being kidnapped and examined by three tall aliens with large eyes.

Evidence of Aliens

It is difficult to prove that aliens have visited Earth. Many people try to photograph spaceships. These photos often turn out to be of everyday objects, however, like airplanes.

One famous incident had several **eyewitnesses** but no evidence. According to members of the Sutton family, a flying saucer landed near their house in 1955. Aliens came out and peered into their windows. They climbed onto the roof of the house. The terrified family tried shooting the aliens. Yet their bullets had no effect.

Afterward, the Sutton family members all claimed they saw the aliens. There were bullet holes, but investigators could find no evidence of aliens.

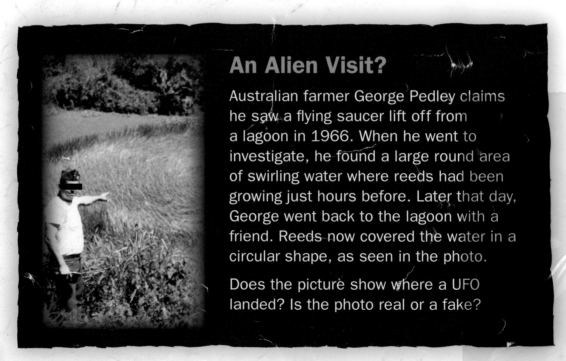

An Alien Visit?

Australian farmer George Pedley claims he saw a flying saucer lift off from a lagoon in 1966. When he went to investigate, he found a large round area of swirling water where reeds had been growing just hours before. Later that day, George went back to the lagoon with a friend. Reeds now covered the water in a circular shape, as seen in the photo.

Does the picture show where a UFO landed? Is the photo real or a fake?

The Roswell Crash

Some alien-believers think that the United States government is trying to hide evidence of UFOs. The most famous case of a UFO "**cover-up**" happened in 1947 outside Roswell, New Mexico.

William Brazel heard an explosion during a storm. The next day, he found some strange metal wreckage. Another man claimed he had found a crashed UFO and four alien bodies in the same area.

The U.S. Air Force removed the wreckage. A few days later, they reported that it was a crashed weather balloon. Official reports later said that there had been no UFO and no dead aliens. Still, many people believe that a UFO crashed near Roswell.

Rendlesham Forest Incident

In 1980, an incident similar to Roswell occurred in England in Rendlesham Forest. Several people, over a three-day period, reported seeing moving lights and a metal spaceship between two air force bases. The lights were later blamed on a nearby lighthouse. However, many eyewitnesses think the British Ministry of Defense tried to hide the story.

17

Alien Hoaxes

Many people truly believe in aliens. However, there are also people who make up alien stories to fool believers. These fake alien stories are called **hoaxes**.

Many photographers have admitted to creating pictures of homemade "spaceships" and tinfoil-covered "spacemen." Some pranksters have gone even further.

In 1974, people in Carbondale, Pennsylvania, claimed they saw a fireball go over a lake. Later, a boy admitted to throwing a lantern into the water.

Starting in the 1960s, several Spaniards received letters supposedly from aliens from the planet Ummo. In 1992, psychologist Jose Luis Jordan Pena admitted to starting the hoax.

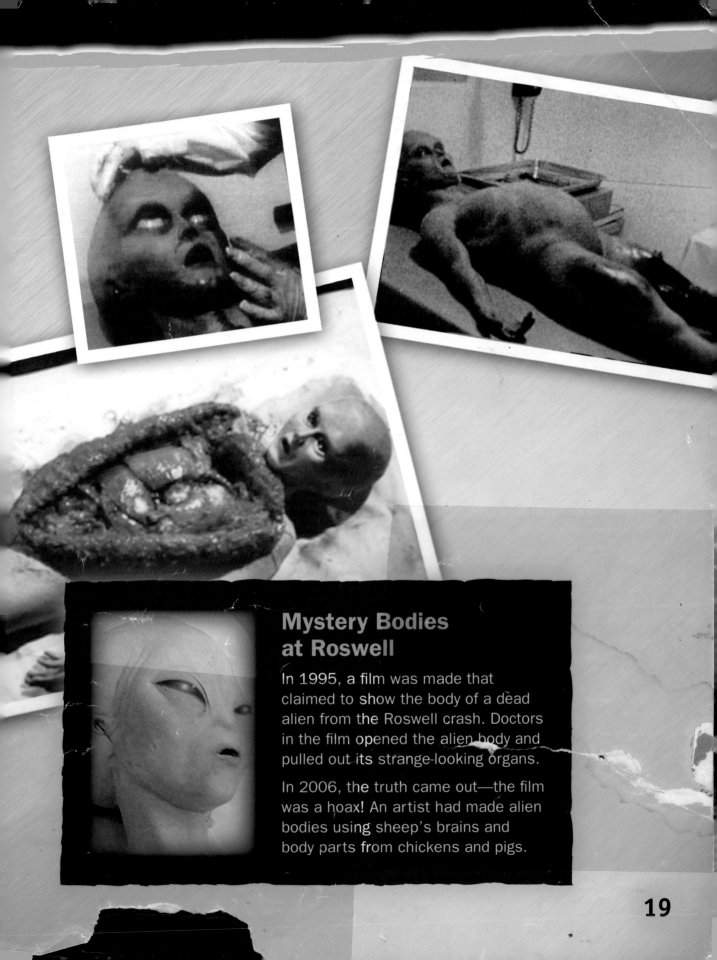

Mystery Bodies at Roswell

In 1995, a film was made that claimed to show the body of a dead alien from the Roswell crash. Doctors in the film opened the alien body and pulled out its strange-looking organs.

In 2006, the truth came out—the film was a hoax! An artist had made alien bodies using sheep's brains and body parts from chickens and pigs.

Hot Spots

Where is the best place to find aliens? Some places in the world are UFO "hot spots." These are areas where UFO and alien sightings are common.

Brazil has more UFO sightings than anywhere else in the world. In 1980, the town of Tres Coroas was terrorized for 20 days by hovering UFOs.

In Russia, a remote area near the Ural mountains is known as the M-triangle. Local people in the M-triangle describe strange lights in the sky. They have also reported meeting glowing aliens in the forest.

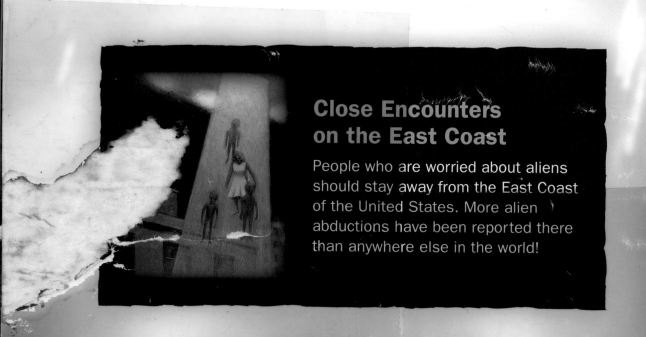

Close Encounters on the East Coast

People who are worried about aliens should stay away from the East Coast of the United States. More alien abductions have been reported there than anywhere else in the world!

Since ancient times, people have reported seeing strange objects, lights in the sky, and mysterious, non-human creatures. One of the first sightings occurred around 1450 BC. Egyptians saw several large "circles of fire" in the sky over several days. The circles rose higher and eventually disappeared.

On August 7, AD 1566, a student in Basel, Switzerland, reported seeing "many large, black globes in the air." He said they were moving before the sun at great speed and turning against each other as if fighting.

Incidents like these happened so long ago that it is difficult for experts to explain them. Were they due to optical illusions or real aliens?

Ancient Astronauts

In some Australian myths, the world was created by spirits called Wandjina. They came to Earth in flying ships from other worlds. Wandjina paintings show figures with halos around their heads. Could these halos be the helmets from space suits?

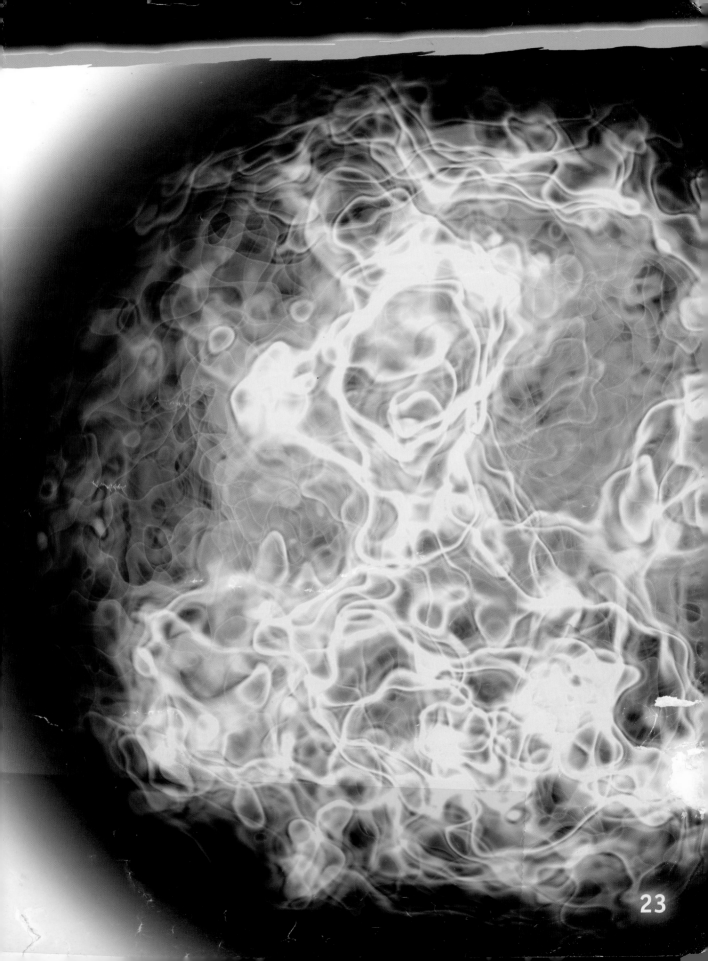

23

Alien Fiction

Many authors of science-fiction books and stories have imagined what would happen if humans and aliens met. One of the first stories about aliens visiting Earth was "Micromégas." The French writer Voltaire wrote it in the 1750s. In the story, two giants come to Earth from outer space.

In John Wyndham's *The Day of the Triffids* (1951), killer plants from outer space take over the world. In Douglas Adams's *The Hitchhiker's Guide to the Galaxy* (1979), aliens destroy Earth to make way for a new highway through space!

H. G. Wells's book *The War of the Worlds* (1898) describes a Martian invasion of Earth. In the end, a common human germ defeats these aliens.

Friendly Aliens

Not all fictional extraterrestrials are hostile. In Arthur C. Clarke's *Childhood's End* (1953), a wise alien saves the human race from a war. In Murray Leinster's *First Contact* (1945), humans and aliens communicate by radio and create a language they both understand.

A scene from the movie
War of the Worlds (2005)

Movie Aliens

In the movies, aliens love to attack humans! In the very first science-fiction film, *A Trip to the Moon* (1902), exploding moon-men chase astronauts.

Many 1950s movies, such as *The Blob* (1958), feature bizarre aliens. In *The Blob*, a meteor carries a giant monster to Earth. It looks like a huge blob of raspberry jam. On Earth, it spreads out and absorbs everyone who gets in its way!

In movies such as *Close Encounters of the Third Kind* (1977) and *E.T.: The Extra-Terrestrial* (1982), the aliens are gentle and peaceful. The alien in *E.T.* befriends a boy who helps him find his way home. In *Men in Black* (1997), some of the aliens are funny creatures just trying to blend in with life on Earth.

MIIB
(Men in Black II)

THIRD-EYE GUY   TENDRILS   MOSH DULO   EYE GUY   CORN FACE

Exploring the Universe

In films and TV shows such as *Star Wars* and *Star Trek*, brave human explorers meet strange creatures. They find many different types of extraterrestrials all over the galaxy. Some of them are kind and intelligent beings. Others are terrifying monsters that gobble up spaceship crews.

IFOs

Thousands of UFOs are reported every year. People get very excited about them because they believe they prove that aliens exist. However, most of the UFO sightings can be explained by weather or by human-made objects.

Many UFO sightings are actually IFOs (Identified Flying Objects). IFOs include low-flying planes, balloons, and **satellites**. Sometimes they are top-secret test planes.

Some IFOs are meteors. Others are strangely-shaped clouds (like the one in this picture), which look like flying saucers. It is very hard to prove a real UFO sighting, especially when pictures are fuzzy or the object appears to be far away.

Freaks of Nature

Natural wonders such as the aurora borealis can also create dramatic effects in the sky. The lights of the aurora borealis can be seen in the sky near the Arctic Circle. They are made by natural electricity in the air.

Another example of dramatic effects in the sky is ball lightning. When this kind of lightning strikes, orange, yellow, or white globes float just above the ground. They can also explode, like a bomb.

Do Aliens Exist?

It is hard to prove whether aliens exist. If they do, they have probably been visiting Earth for thousands of years already. So don't panic—they haven't destroyed the planet yet!

Scientists are looking into space for other planets that can grow life. The Hubble Space Telescope has shown that there are billions of galaxies like ours. So there is a very good chance that living creatures exist somewhere else in the **universe**.

Can these living creatures travel to other planets? Have they visited Earth? People still disagree on the answers. Perhaps someday scientists will prove that alien life does exist!

Life on Mars

There may be alien life somewhere in our **solar system**. In 2004, two robot explorers were sent to Mars to look for signs of water. Where there is water, there is usually life.

NASA (National Aeronautics and Space Administration) scientists believe there is a strong chance that life exists on Mars. They think it's hidden in underground caves. These Martians won't be scary monsters, but tiny **microbes**.

Glossary

abduction (ab-DUK-shun) taking someone away against his or her will; kidnapping

astronomers (uh-STRON-uh-murz) scientists who study outer space

cover-up (KUHV-ur-UHP) when people try to hide something or make it look like something never happened

extraterrestrials (ek-struh-tuh-RESS-tree-uhlz) beings from other planets or parts of the universe

eyewitnesses (EYE-WIT-niss-iz) people who saw something with their own eyes

flying saucer (FLYE-ing SAW-sur) a type of UFO that looks like a big disk or a metal saucer flying through the air

galaxy (GAL-uhk-see) a large group of stars

hoaxes (HOHKS-iz) tricks that make people believe something that is not true

hypnosis (hip-NOH-siss) the use of special words and actions to make people fall into a sleep-like state in which they can be made to remember things they forgot when they were awake

meteors (MEE-tee-urz) rocks or other small objects from space that burn and cause a streak of light to be seen as they fly into Earth's atmosphere

microbes (MYE-krohbs) tiny, simple living things

NASA (NAS-ah) (National Aeronautics and Space Administration) an organization in the United States that studies space and builds spacecraft

paralyzed (PA-ruh-lized) unable to move one's body

satellites (SAT-uh-lites) spacecraft that circle Earth as they send and receive radio and TV signals

sightings (SITE-ingz) occasions when people have seen something

solar system (SOH-lur SISS-tuhm) a star and all the planets, moons, meteors, and other objects that travel around it

UFOs (YOO EF OHZ) (Unidentified Flying Objects) objects seen in the air that cannot be explained by human activities or nature

universe (YOO-nuh-vurss) everything that exists on Earth and in the rest of space

Index

Adams, Douglas 24

Alexander the Great 6

aurora borealis 29

ball lightning 29

The Blob 26

British Ministry of Defense 17

Childhood's End 24

Clarke, Arthur C. 24

Close Encounters of the Third Kind 26

The Day of the Triffids 24

E.T.: The Extra-Terrestrial 4, 26

First Contact 24

gray aliens 10

The Hitchhiker's Guide to the Galaxy 24

Hubble Space Telescope 30

Hynek, J. Allen 8

IFOs 28–29

Leinster, Murray 24

Men in Black 26

"Micromégas" 24

M-triangle 20

Nordic aliens 10

Roswell crash 16–17, 19

Roswell film 19

Star Trek 27

Star Wars 27

Sutton family 14

A Trip to the Moon 26

U.S. Air Force 16

Voltaire 24

The War of the Worlds 24

Wells, H. G. 24

Wyndham, John 24